Michael Nyman

Manhatta

for Soprano Voice and Bass Clarinet

(2003/2013)

This is the composer's arrangement of a piece commissioned by the Eos Orchestra and originally scored for large ensemble. The premiere was given on 24 April 2003 by the Eos Orchestra at the New York Society for Ethical Culture.

Duration: *circa* 7½ minutes

Text from 'Mannahatta'
by Walt Whitman

Manhatta

for Soprano Voice and Bass Clarinet

Michael Nyman

- cient,

I see that the word of my

ci - ty is that word from of old, Be - cause I see

that word nest - ed in nests of wat - er - bays, su -

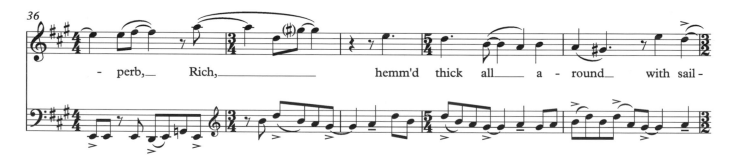

- perb, Rich, hemm'd thick all a - round with sail -

- ships and steam - ships, an is - land six - - teen

miles long, sol - id found - ed,

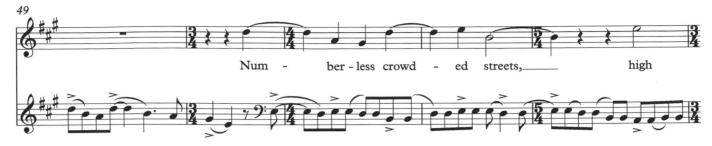

Num - ber - less crowd - ed streets,_____ high

growths of i - ron, slen - der,_____ strong,_____ light,_____

_____ splen - did - ly_____ up - ris - ing_____ to - wards clear

skies,

Tides swift and

am - ple,_____ well - loved by me,_____ to - ward

goods, the man - ly__ race of dri-vers of hor - ses,_____ the__

brown - faced sail - ors,

The sum - mer air,_____ the bright sun

shin - ing, and the sail - ing clouds a - loft,___

The win - ter snows, the sleigh - bells,_____ the bro - ken ice__

__ in the riv - er, pass-ing a - long up_____ or down__ with the flood-tide or

4

Bass Clarinet in B♭

Manhatta
for Soprano Voice and Bass Clarinet

Text from Manahatta
by Walt Whitman

Michael Nyman

ebb - tide,____

The mech - an - ics_ of___ the ci - ty,____ the

mas - ters,___ well - form'd, beau - ti - ful - faced, look - ing you_ straight

____ in the eyes,

Trot - toirs throng'd, ve - hi - cles, Broad -

- way,___ the____ wo - men,___ the shops____

and shows,____

A mil - lion peo -

- ple — man - ners free and su - perb —

op - en____ voi - ces____ —

hos - pi - ta - li - ty —

the most cour - a - geous____ and friend - ly young men,

My ci - ty's fit___ and no - ble name re - sumed,___

Choice___ ab - or - ig - in - al name,___

with mar - vel - lous___ beau - - ty, mean -

- ing,___ A rock - y___ found - ed is - land___ —

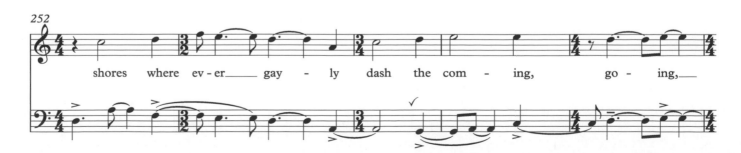

shores where ev - er___ gay - ly dash the com - ing, go - ing,___

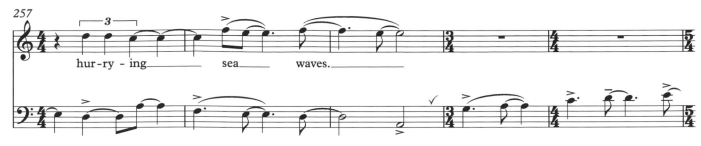

hur-ry - ing_____ sea____ waves._____

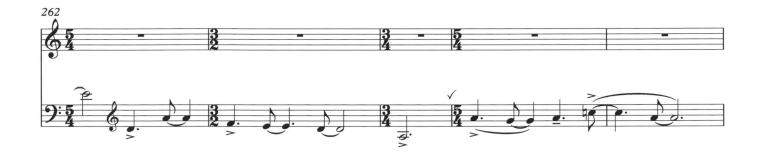

ah_____

sim. al fine